AF481155

# Women As Second-Class Citizens to Men

## Ancient Greece Kids Book 6th Grade Children's Ancient History

Speedy Publishing LLC

40 E. Main St. #1156

Newark, DE 19711

www.speedypublishing.com

Copyright 2017

In this book, we're going to talk about the role of women in Ancient Greece. So, let's get right to it!

# Aphrodite

# ANCIENT GREEK WOMEN

During Ancient times, the Greek people made offerings to and worshipped both gods and goddesses. Although the goddesses were not as powerful as the gods, they still were seen as strong. Sometimes they were depicted as clever enough to beat out their male counterparts in competition, as the goddess

Athena did when she beat out the sea god Poseidon. She won this competition by delivering an olive tree compared to Poseidon's seawater. The citizens chose her gift as the best and subsequently she became the protector for a new city that was eventually named after her, Athens.

ATHENA

SAPPHO

Unfortunately, this viewpoint of women as being strong and intelligent didn't hold true in their day-to-day lives. Human women were not regarded in the same way as goddesses and were definitely considered second-class citizens compared to men.

This treatment affected every area of their lives and they were largely confined to their homes. For the most part, women were not equal partners in their marriages. Men often treated them like children.

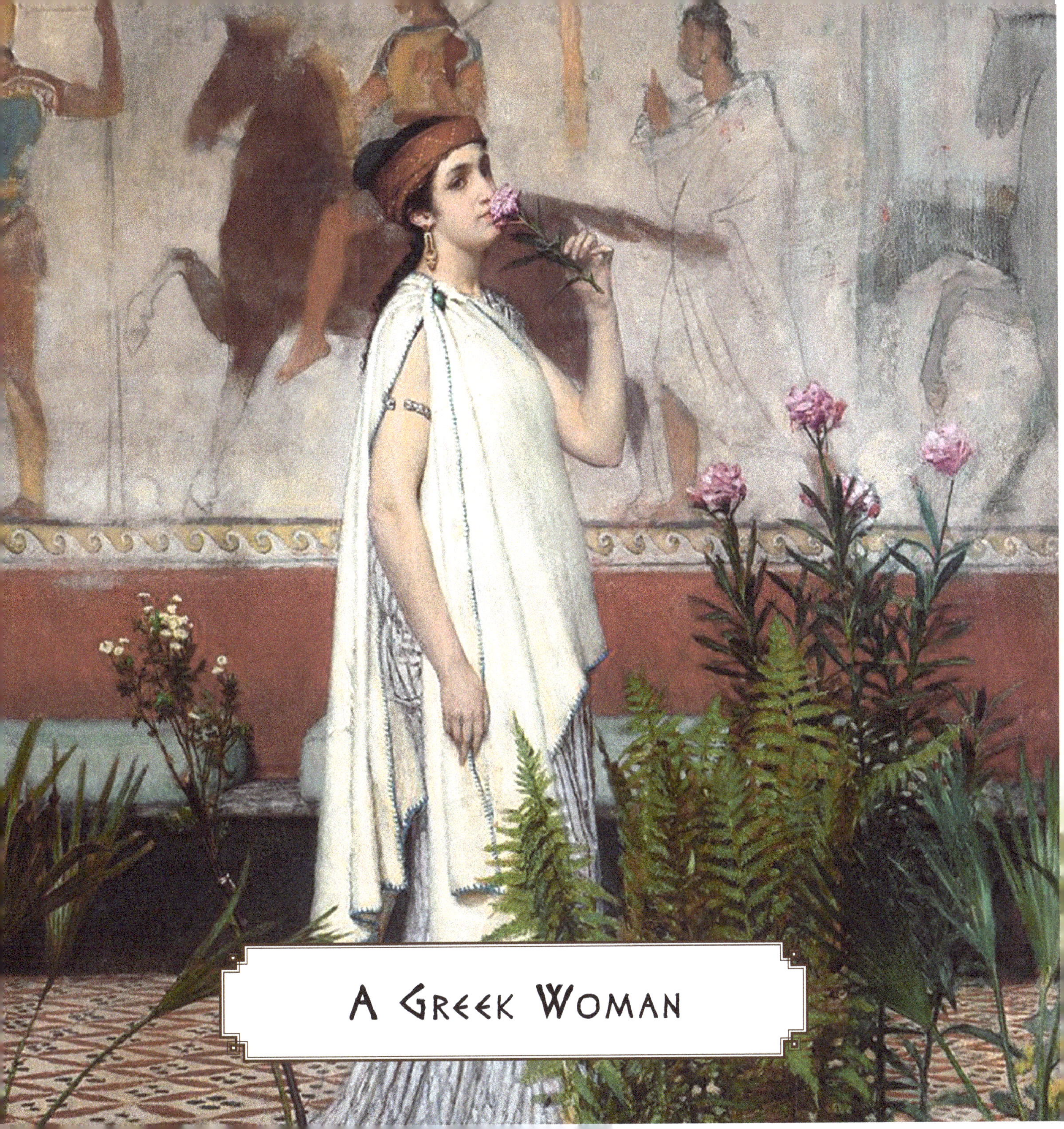

A Greek Woman

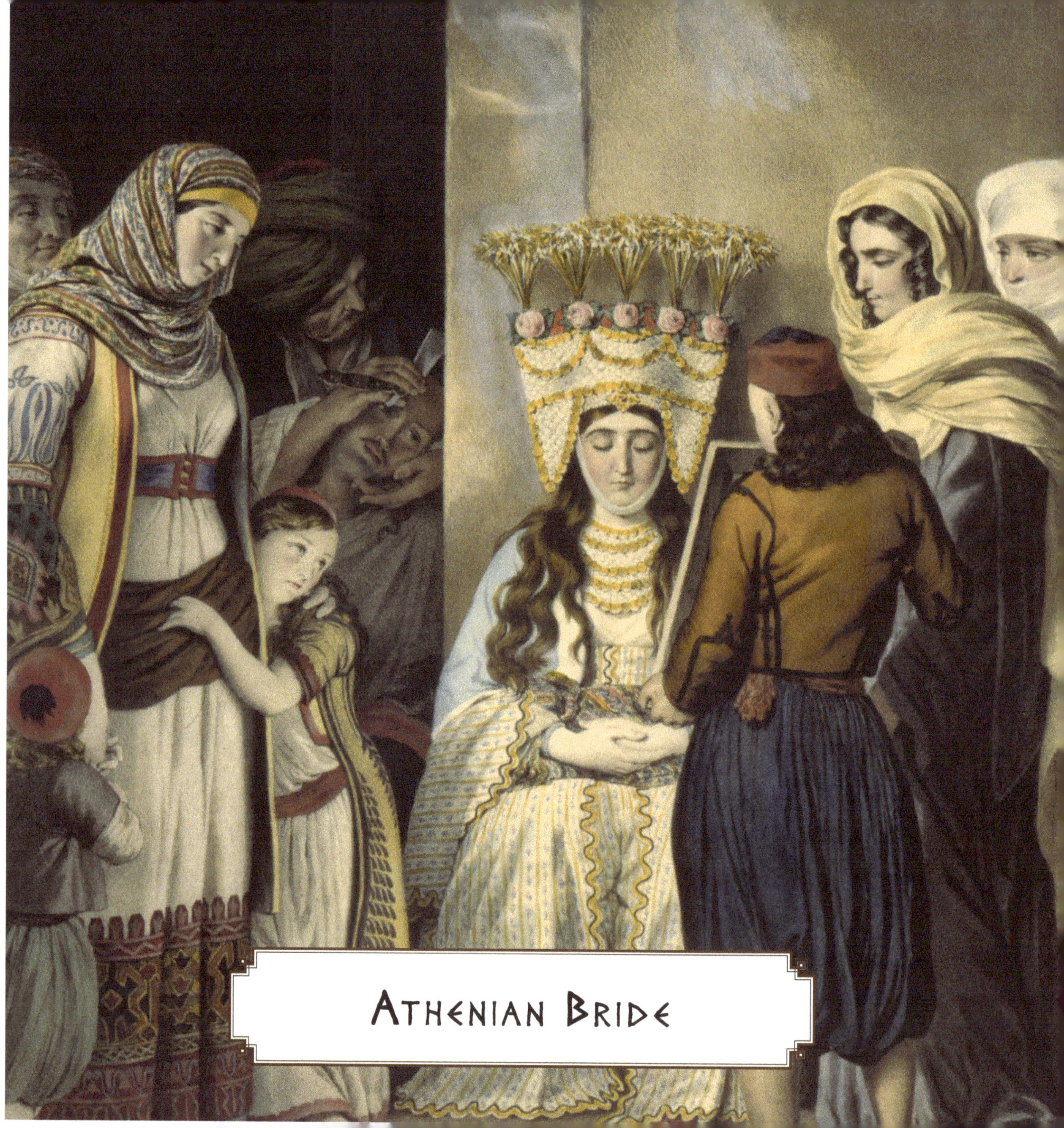

# ATHENIAN BRIDE

# GREEK WOMEN AND MARRIAGE

In most countries around the world today, women and men marry primarily for romantic love. However, during the time of Ancient Greece, this wasn't how people decided to join in marriage. Marriages were predetermined by the father of the household who would be responsible for matchmaking his daughters to men who could provide for them.

These arranged marriages generally happened when girls were around the age of 15. This seems young, but at that time the average length of a person's life was about 35-40 years. The women had little to no say in terms of the husband selected for them. Many times young women were married to older men who had property and could care for them.

A young Greek Woman

GIRLS WERE RULED BY THEIR FATHERS

Prior to marriage, girls were ruled by their fathers. After they were married, their husbands had control over them. Greek men were quite vain about their ability to reason and think. Although they admired women for their beauty as well as for their abilities as wives and mothers, for the most part they considered them to be too emotional to be considered equal partners in business or life.

# THE GREEK HOME

Usually the top floors of a Greek home were reserved for the women and children of the household. This is where they lived and slept. Women and men didn't share their meals together. The women and children were not allowed to go into the room where men entertained and had dinner with their male friends.

Greek Homes

They had freedom of movement within the house with the exception of that room. In some city-states, such as Athens, women were often not allowed to leave their houses. Men didn't want other men to have access to their wives.

# Wealthy Woman

# WEALTHY WOMEN

Women that were married to wealthy men had slaves to do menial tasks around the house, run errands, and take care of the grounds. Wealthy women might have been able to take occasional trips to visit family and friends, but for the most part they stayed at home.

Their role was to make sure the household was managed and maintained. They were also prized for being able to give birth to sons who would be heirs to the

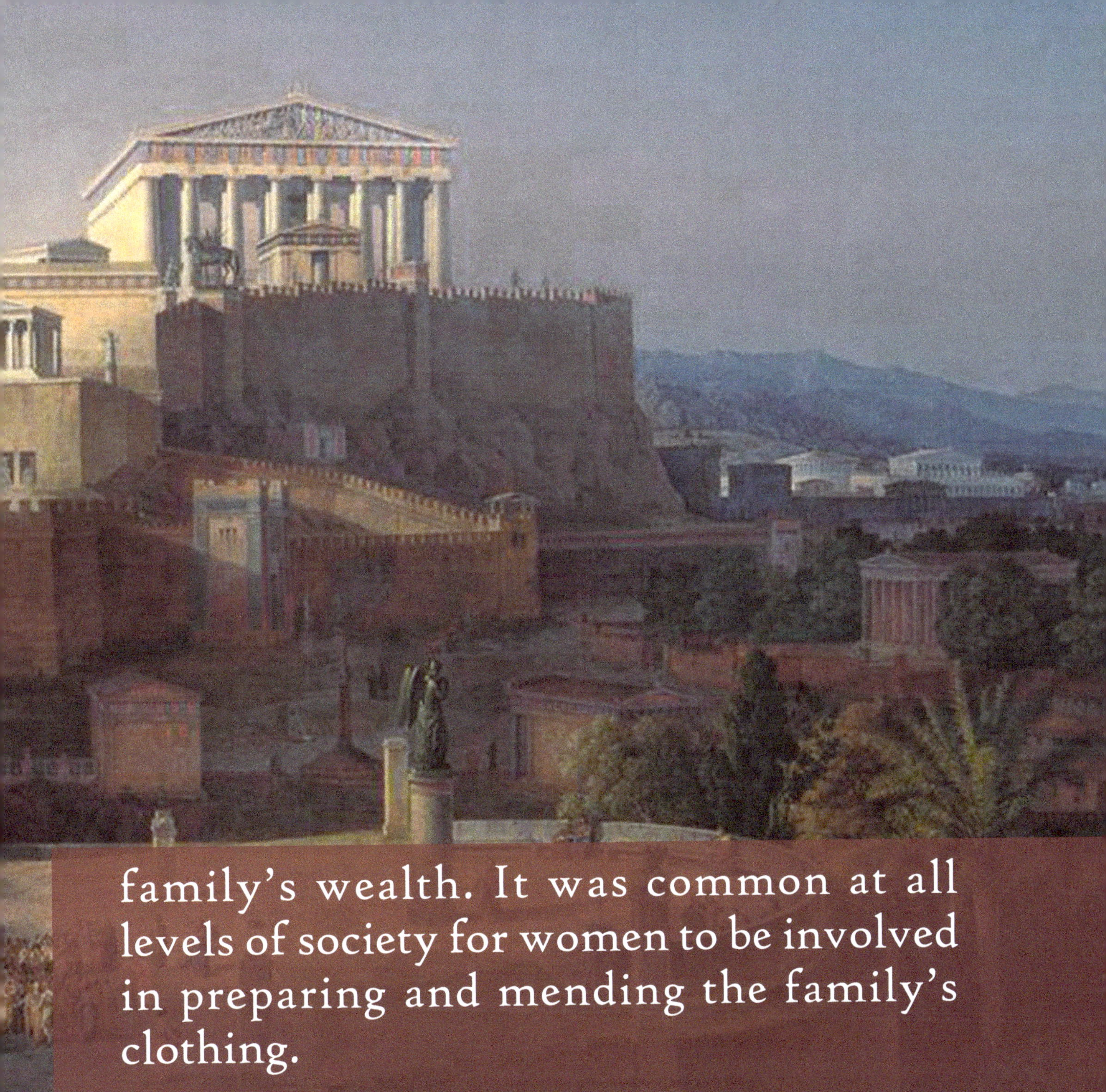

family's wealth. It was common at all levels of society for women to be involved in preparing and mending the family's clothing.

# Neoclassical young ladies

# MIDDLE CLASS WOMEN

In many cases middle class women and poor women had more "freedoms" than wealthy women. Due to economic necessity, middle class women sometimes took jobs outside the home to make the needed income to sustain their families.

They found work as shopkeepers or as servants for rich families. Some women took over the management of inns or made cloth or did sewing for a living. They had to leave their homes in order to go on errands, get water, and purchase items and food for their households if they didn't have slaves to do this for them.

SERVANTS

WOMEN LIVED AND WORKED ON FARMS

# POOR WOMEN

Many women lived and worked on farms. Most farming families were relatively poor. In addition to their household duties, they would have worked hard in the fields by harvesting olives, fruits, and vegetables.

# SLAVE WOMEN

Slave women were considered to be the lowest class of all in Ancient Greece. Male slaves had more rights than they did, simply because they were men.

TIRED YOUNG MAID

Spartan Woman Giving Shield to Her Son

# Women in the City-State of Sparta

In Sparta, men were so concerned with warfare that they didn't have time for much else. As a result, women had more independence than they did in other regions of Greece and they had freedom of movement throughout the city. Women were more admired than in Athens for their ability to be "mothers of Spartan warriors."

Around 400 BC, two-fifths of the property in Sparta was women-owned. This was very unusual because in other city-states, all property had to be handed down through the men in the family, from father to son and women had very few property rights.

Spartan woman and her slave

There were other differences in Sparta as well. Girls were allowed to attend schools run by the government and participate in athletics. Of course, it was still true that the women who gave birth to male heirs were the most highly regarded. Almost all the women in Sparta had slaves to do the heavy work in their households.

# DID WOMEN HAVE ANY LEGAL RIGHTS?

The city-states of Greece differed in the type of rights women had. Ironically, although the city of Athens was named after a strong goddess, they didn't allow women many rights. In Athens, they couldn't actively participate in any activity related to governing or voting. In almost all cases, they were not allowed to have property of their own either.

# Feast of Thesmophoria

# THE FEAST OF THESMOPHORIA

Women were able to occasionally attend religious festivals that were designed to worship the gods and goddesses. Sometimes these events were held inside temples where only women worshipped.

The feast of Thesmophoria was a special religious festival that was enjoyed by married women and their children. It was designed to honor the goddess of the harvest, Persephone, and her beloved daughter Demeter. The festival was held in many cities throughout Greece. In Athens, the women gathered on an outdoor hill called Pnyx, which was generally used for men's political discussions.

They fasted for one complete day to show their devotion. Then, they did something unusual. They hurled insults and clever witty comments back and forth to each other.

They felt the gods and goddesses were listening and it would be entertaining for them. The more

entertaining it was for these deities, the better the crops would grow. This festival provided a social outlet for women who were taking care of very young children and were otherwise housebound.

# BEAUTY AND FASHION

Women with very pale complexions were seen as the most beautiful, since Greeks had olive complexions for the most part. When the weather was sunny, women would remain under the roofed portions of their courtyards so their skin wouldn't get burned or too deep in color. Many art objects of that era show women resting in their courtyards.

A WOMAN FROM ATHENS

To make their skin even fairer, women would apply white lead to their skin. They didn't have any idea how toxic lead was at that time. Chalk was used sometimes but it wore off fast, so lead was preferred. They used dark powder to emphasize their eyes and they connected their eyebrows together, which was in fashion at the time.

Wealthy women kept their long hair in braids, which were sometimes piled on their heads. They wore tiaras or headbands made of metal to keep these elaborate hairstyles in place.

# FASCINATING FACTS ABOUT WOMEN IN ANCIENT GREECE

Stoicism was an Ancient Greek philosophy that supported the idea that men and women were equals in all things.

When a woman gave birth to a daughter when a son was hoped for, it was a cause for intense shame. Sometimes unwanted girls were abandoned.

In the city-state of Athens, women's spending was controlled. They were only allowed to buy or sell a very specific small amount. The value they were allowed to buy was called a "medimnos" and was measured by 52 liters of grain. This value gave them the power to buy and sell modest amounts of food or small objects. They were shut out of major business transactions.

O ne of the most important positions a woman could hold in Ancient Greece was the position of priestess to a goddess of Greek mythology. A priestess was supposedly able to communicate directly with the goddess she worshipped.

Women were not allowed to attend the Olympics. If a married woman was caught on site, she could be put to death.

Now you know more about how women were considered second class citizens compared to men during the time of the Ancient Greek civilization. You can find more Ancient History books from Baby Professor by searching the website of your favorite book retailer.

Visit

BABY PROFESSOR
EDUCATION KIDS

www.BabyProfessorBooks.com

to download Free Baby Professor eBooks
and view our catalog of new and exciting
Children's Books